The Pond

a small book about making big changes

The Pond
a small book about making big changes

John K Kriger

Contributing Editor - Megan Baillie

Megan Baillie

With a diverse background in marketing and higher education, Megan provides editing services in the United States and Canada. She holds a Bachelors degree in Communications and a Masters Degree in Leadership and Public Administration. She currently lives in British Columbia, Canada with her husband.

Dedication

This book is dedicated to all those who have allowed me to stand on their shoulders so that I could see what was possible in my life. I thank my wife for believing in me, even when she could not "see" where I was headed and yet she still backed me.

I thank my kids who taught me what a difference listening can mean, the power of being present and their willingness to play along with me as I worked through being a parent. I guess they know by now that I didn't have any idea what I was doing. They seemed to be able to learn from my faults as well as my talents, becoming adults that I cherish and enjoy. They have, and continue to teach me more than they will ever know.

I thank my parents for giving me the best they had to give. Today I recognize the sacrifices they made and without their examples, I would not be where I am today. Thank you to Uncle Ken and Aunt Eva. While they are not with us today, they still embody the totality of the energy of life so they will be in our hearts forever. And finally, Kay with her faith, and Irish spirit showed me that nothing can stand in your way when you believe strongly enough to make it happen.

And I thank God for not giving up on me when I was tempted to give up on myself. Since I am still here, I guess he is not done with me yet. I thank him for the gift of silent serenity that eludes me so often and yet presents itself constantly when I can just be still enough to accept it.

Miracles often happen
in the silence of the mind,
that others sometimes call
nothing...........

Introduction

For years I have used variations of The Pond in trainings and lectures to describe how groups and organizations develop, function and dysfunction. From its meager beginning, to its near death by stagnation, The Pond serves as a mirror for self examination for families, groups, and organization to begin identifying with the animals, in their processes, and behaviors. As in any system, a healthy balance of its members and organization are vital. As with the inhabitants of The Pond, our actions take us either toward or away from our goals, often without us noticing how our actions impact our outcomes. The Pond serves as a story of hope, because as long as there is willingness to productively engage one another, we can grow.

When we can stop reacting and needing to be right, we empty ourselves of certainty and defensive blindness, entering into the space where real magic happens. As we seek greater options, we can more securely examine ourselves and begin asking the vital question of "what is possible?" with an open heart.

I believe out of habit and expedience, we continue utilizing problem solving models, negatively focusing our attention, and derailing us from creating the world we really want. It is time for us to take greater responsibility for making ourselves, our organizations, and the world a better place. As I've watched my children grow and now my grand children, I realize the accountability for making this world a better place is mine, as it is yours. It begins with me learning tools, methods, and taking action to improving and creating the world around me. In this small way I can begin to generate more positive energy, kinder interactions and hope for the future. I only pray we can begin to take the higher road, treating others with kindness when anger seems easier. Seeking understanding when being right would seem more expedient. And realizing this world is not ours to do with what we want, but rather a sacred space in time that we have been entrusted to guard, nurture, and protect. I hope you enjoy this little book as much as we have enjoyed writing and developing it.

One

"All too often they moved in, settled down, and stayed because it was comfortable and their needs were met."

Once upon a time, there was a small, gently running stream. It started as a little spring in the ground that continually ran with fresh water. At first it seeped as if it were an idea whose time had come, gently bubbling up from the earth's center. Soon it began to dribble, then gush and flow more steadily where it joined more small streams forming the headwaters of an impressively crisp flow of water. From this beginning, it flowed for miles, eventually feeding larger streams, until it merged with a large river flowing into the ocean. As the summer rains fed the stream, it began to run faster and faster, moving everything within its path. Soon the water began to dig out the soil it encountered, heaving it into its turbulent current, creating deep pockets in the ground, making the stream deeper, richer, and more serene. Very soon, a large pond was formed.

Fish quickly found the streams leading into the pond and the fresh, cold, rich water. As more fish discovered the pond, they decided to stay. Aquatic plants began to grow in the enriched environment created by the fish, nutrients, sunlight, and cool water. Soon frogs located the pond and decided it was also a great place to raise their families. Tadpoles began to hatch in the small tributaries formed at the pond's edge.

As the pond grew in depth, width, and experience, it began to offer its new inhabitants more varied opportunities for growth and enrichment. New, fresh, vibrant waters constantly refreshed the pond, offering food, hiding places, and stimulation. The support within the environment encouraged access to a variety of species. All too often they moved in, settled down, and stayed because it was comfortable and their needs were met.

15   The Pond

In the slow, circulating pools, young fish grew in safe and supportive nests. Frogs hid in the weeds that provided them shelter and safety. At the water line shaded hollows amongst the tree roots acted as incubators for the fresh young weeds growing along them. Sunlight filtered down through the weeds warming the pools that supported the young fish and amphibians. Tadpoles and small fish chased each other, like children playing tag, amongst the roots and stems, unconcerned about danger in the dense cover.

As the young fish used the weed beds for safety, the larger and older fish drifted slowly into the deeper waters to find room to hunt and grow. Bass lay in the deeper waters to escape the streaming rays of sun, nestled up against the dark sullen hulks of fallen trees along the bottom. Pike and larger fish entered the deep waters and sank down into the cold to escape the heat. The deep waters allowed bottom-feeders to find scraps the larger fish dropped, in addition to succulent freshwater clams and mussels who had taken up residence in the soft oatmeal-like mud. An abundance of turtles lay sunning on bits of floating wood, while others silently dove to find small aquatic meals.

A clan of beavers, looking for tender saplings, wandered through the woods, drawn by the fresh scent of clean water. The beavers found the tender young growth of fresh seedlings quite to their liking, so they built a hut, called a "mound" in the shallow end of the pond and took up housekeeping there, basking in sun and enjoying the quiet of this newly discovered oasis.

The Pond

Birds of all kinds came in droves to the now large pond. Hawks, falcons, and even an occasional eagle would lazily soar high above the pond. Looking like disinterested tourists, they meticulously scanned the water's surface, looking for fish that were careless enough to go near the calm surface waters. Cranes majestically stalked the edges like wilting flowers, slowly bending forward until suddenly snapping a small fish or frog from the shallows. Ducks and geese began raising their broods in the tall soft grasses now surrounding the pond. The tall marsh grasses blew in the soft summer breeze, like sheets hung to dry, billowing out to provide safety and shelter for a myriad of wildlife flourishing at its roots. With purposeful determination the Seagulls picked at the shells washed ashore, keeping the sands clean and free of dead fish and decay

Muskrats, beavers, mice, and even mink found the shoreline that, with its ruts and hollows, provided a place of safety. In fact, they all felt safe and happy here. The pond provided each of them with the environment that felt right, like they belonged, and supplied them each with the sustenance needed to grow healthy and strong.

Two

*"Unless you have at least three
generations in the mud, you don't really
belong here!"*

Now as it happens, one summer the beavers that had taken up residence near the far end, decided they liked the pond so much they would keep it just the way it was. The beavers didn't socialize much with the other animals. In fact, they liked their huts as far away from the land's edge as they could be, and still get ashore to get twigs. They knew they couldn't go into deeper waters for it would not sustain the large mounds they built. In their estimation, the pond was the most perfect place to live and the beavers could make such a judgment because they had been there from the beginning. In fact, they felt entitled to their end of the pond since they had been there so much longer than any other animals. Now it was true that the beavers wouldn't venture too far from their mounds anyway, but they didn't think they had to see anything else to be thankful for what they had. You'd always hear them say, "You don't have to go too far to know what you've got," to any suggestions of travel. In fact, the beavers believed that you could only truly come to call a place home by staying put generation after generation, so the years went by.

The beavers would welcome newcomers to the pond with the strange expression, "Unless you have at least three generations in the mud, you don't really belong here!" The mud the beavers were referring to was the beaver's way of explaining death. They believed that when a beaver died, they would simply float away and become part of the dirt. And since the beavers used the dirt and mud to build their mounds, they would be keeping their family, and their memories, with them forever. This belief only deepened their sense of home in the pond.

The beavers saw just how wonderful their home was and often took time to bask in the sun, and enjoy the invigorating, slightly cooler nights. They'd snuggle up in beaver comfort during the winter months and fully enjoy the culinary delicacies the pond provided during the warm summer. The beavers truly appreciated all the pond provided them.

As generations of beavers filled the mound, they would listen to the elders talk about their journey to the pond and how they each made it home. The eldest beavers would describe how important it was to build strong walls and structures so their dams would stand forever. After they were built, the mounds had to be constantly repaired and renewed. This is because the beavers believed that unwanted changes could be delayed by constantly working to keep things the same. Whenever they saw any sign of disrepair, it was essential they go fix it right away. Failure to do so would threaten their very existence. If things changed, life itself would suffer. You see, the beavers believed they were superior to the other animals since they could swim on top of and under water, walk on land, clear forests with their teeth, and build on the very mud of their ancestors. "No other animal is as smart or as advanced as we are," they'd say. According to the beavers, they were entitled to be happy, despite what the other animals said. They knew best what had to be done. Of course, that was the way it had always been done.

"Getting your head full of new ideas was dangerous," mother beavers would warn their cubs. "After all, it's all about the kids."

As long as mother beavers spoke about what was best for the kids, they could avoid any arguments that might surface. No one dislikes kids or wants to appear foolish enough to be accused of not caring about future generations. The beavers were clever animals and knew that by using the children to back up their good intentions, they could rationalize their ideas and deflect any contrary opinions. The beavers also constantly promoted the rules, and with their history at the pond, the beavers quickly became important to the rest of the community. Not surprising, the beavers were also quick to reprimand anyone who failed to conform to their ways of thinking. After all, when you're "right," you're justified in your actions!

This meant the beavers were pretty much allowed to do anything they wanted. No one wanted to appear foolish or be ridiculed for questioning the beavers' actions or reasoning. And being right was important to the beavers. If they were wrong, they would be considered weak and vulnerable. "The hut is the most valid source of information," believed the beavers. "You should be careful of those who think, act, or look differently." Their motto was, "Keep yourself safe." The beavers could tolerate the other animals because they had been there so long. But while they had become used to them, there was still doubt in a lot of their interactions.

For a long time, these differences seemed to go unspoken and relatively unnoticed—that is, until the evening of the big storm.

Three

*"Shouldn't we have a plan for what it
is exactly we're doing?"*

The animals could tell something unusual was about to happen. The summer days had been extremely hot and the humidity hung in the air. The deer found themselves going to the pond to drink far more often than normal. They even waded out into the water to cool off. The grass was dying in the open areas and the plant-eaters were competing for what was left of the shade. The water level of the pond had lowered, causing the mink, muskrats, and beavers to begin voicing concerns for the state of the pond. The eagles and hawks had changed their hunting habits, now flying much lower, causing the mound builders to become concerned for their smaller children's safety. The smaller land rodents, frogs, and other smaller animals also felt and expressed their concern.

Then one evening in late August, the heat wave broke. Strong winds began to blow and the sky turned very dark. The animals knew they were in for a strong storm. They took shelter immediately in trees, dens, bushes, holes, or deep in the pond's waters to ride out the storm. Once the rains began, it rained like it had never rained before. It seemed like the skies opened up and let pour all it had withheld for months. Trees that had held strong for hundreds of years toppled over in the wind. Many animals were killed and others wounded, but as day broke the following morning, the winds subsided and the rain stopped. One by one, the animals cautiously came out to survey the damage. Many dens had been flooded out and a few animals had lost their homes completely.

When the beavers finally came out of their mound, they found the forest had been seriously damaged. Trees had been toppled all over the pond's edge. The beavers could now reach the higher, soft new growth that littered the forest floor, but they were so taken aback by the pond's appearance they didn't even realize there had been a benefit to the storm. "We have to clean this up," one beaver said.

27   The Pond

"We have to get back to things the way they were," said another. The fact that the pond had changed so much so quickly caused the entire pond community to feel out of control and in shock. No one knew what to do about the now devastated pond, and the animals started to become wary of each other.

The beavers spoke amongst themselves about the damage that occurred for quite some time and remembered what their ancestors had said, "No beaver ever lets another animal know their fur is ruffled. Looking good is everything." This was a lesson for the beavers about what could happen if you let things change. "What would we ever do if this pond changed?" they asked with apprehension. The recent damage had brought this possibility screeching into reality. "What if things change?" they asked each other. As they talked they began to expand their thoughts and fears. "If only we could have kept the pond as it was," one beaver said sadly. Fear was something the beavers believed should not be shown. It was an indicator of weakness and showed that their fur was in fact "ruffled."

So the beavers decided to put their fear aside; it was up to them to save the pond since they were the smartest animals in the pond. After all, doing something, even if the other animals didn't like it, was better than doing nothing at all. Most of the beavers decided to no longer speak to the other animals and put their plan into action. They couldn't trust the other animals. "All of this will be worth it, if we save just one of the children!" the parents exclaimed. The beavers rallied around this comment and got to work restoring the pond. "Shouldn't we have a plan for what it is exactly we're doing?" one of the young beavers asked. "There's simply no time for that," replied one of the elders. "If there's any sign of trouble, just make noise and get busy!" And with that they were off to work. But as the beavers started working, a few of the independent-thinking beavers began to talk amongst themselves. They didn't want to cause trouble but something just didn't feel right. After all, as long as any of them could remember, it was the way it had always been done before.

The one thing the beavers did take the time to decide was to agree not to tell the other animals what they were doing. The beavers feared what the animals would think and, worse yet, what they might they do if they disagreed or had a different idea. The other animals might disapprove or try to get involved. To keep on task without letting the other animals know, a small group of beavers met during the day while most of the others were sleeping. "It's not that we don't want their input," the beavers rationalized, "it's just easier to get things done with fewer opinions to consider." During one of their meetings, the beavers decided to build a new dam at the pond's head, so they could better control the water coming into the pond. With light in his eyes, one of the beavers explained, "If we can control the pond itself, we can stop things from ever changing again!"

So, doing what has always worked before, the beavers went right to work building the dam. They cut down saplings despite the fact that their roots kept the banks from eroding and provided homes to muskrats, turtles, and fish. They chewed down large trees that provided shade for hatchlings and prevented overly ambitious weed growth. They also removed the trees the deer used for shelter when they drank at the pond, and that sheltered nesting birds.

Four

"If you're not with us, you're
against us…"

Almost immediately, the animals noticed the difference but each feared that they were the only one to notice so they pretended not to see it. The pond had always been a peaceful place and no one wanted to be a troublemaker. No one wants to cause trouble. Besides, it was okay to speak about trouble from outside the pond, but when it came from within, it was a different story.

The more the pond changed, the more the animals pretended not to see it. But Emin, a middle-aged beaver, who had always been one of the forward thinkers, expressed his concerns of the possibility of water damage to the trees along the original shoreline due to the flooding. But Emin's concerns were immediately dismissed. "If you're not with us, you're against us; a wolf in beaver's clothing!" shouted one of the elders. Emin was deeply hurt by this. He didn't want to create dissension in the mound. The beavers always prided themselves in being able to stick together and although Emin didn't agree, even he certainly didn't want to dishonor the mound. Isolated, Emin felt his loyalty to the mound was being tested. That is until he realized that there were other beavers that felt like he did. "Why do you take that?" asked one of his freethinking friends. "Well," Emin replied, "they've been right as far back as I can remember." And with that they followed the rest of the workers out into the pond for a day of building.

Before too long, all of this pretending made the new-thinking beavers, and many of the other animals, begin to doubt themselves. Doubt made the animals feel unsafe and allowed them to make excuses for pretending. It confused them because they felt funny about what was happening, but they didn't dare say anything. Pretending nothing was happening was just easier to deal with. All the uncertainties and insecurities made the animals began to distrust each other, even within their own schools, flocks, gaggles, and families; especially the beavers. They began to fight and blame each other. The few that did talk, secretly shared their feelings, but felt no one else understood what they were going through. Certainly other ponds didn't have these problems. Eventually, while some animals tried to stay and rebuild their lives, most left to start over at another pond.

As animals began to leave the pond, most of the beavers were patting themselves on the back. They watched the waters run from their new dam into the surrounding meadow making it soggy and the pond larger. "How wonderful this is!" exclaimed the beavers. "We not only stopped losing water, but we have also gained even more now! And with so many of the animals leaving, all this water is ours! Now everyone should be happy!" they exclaimed.

Days after the pond started to grow, several deer stood talking on the edge of the pond as the beavers were on their way home from a day of work. As the beavers walked, they heard the deer complaining about the changes. Annoyed by what they heard, the beavers spoke to each other loudly enough for the deer to overhear, "They're just a bunch of complainers.

The animals who don't like what we're doing just don't understand how good the pond will be because of us." Another beaver chimed in, "If they don't like it, why didn't they do something to fix it?" Hearing the beavers, the deer tried to respond but the beavers were already on their way into the water without waiting for a response.

Five

*"They just knew everyone would want
to celebrate their success."*

It wasn't long before even the beavers began
to realize that the pond was taking on more
water than it could handle. The beavers decided
a work crew should be sent to stop the flow of
water. Because Emin had been defiant enough
to voice his concerns earlier, he was chosen to
fix the problem. Wakcu, an elder and another
new-thinker, spoke up in Emin's defense saying
he didn't want to see Emin go alone. Less
verbal than Emin, Wakcu supported Emin's
efforts and felt he was being treated unfairly.
So Emin and Wakcu swam across the pond and

into the headwaters that fed the pond. Several of the young aspiring leaders and a few elders accompanied them to make sure it was done right.

They had to swim hard to get up stream and Emin and Wakcu hoped their hard work would pacify the beavers, and maybe please the other animals. But when they arrived at the headwaters, they had grave concerns. Knowing the price they'd pay if they failed their assignment, they did whatever they could to stop the water. The beavers were one of the hardest working animals in the pond. They knew this legacy had to be maintained or shame would befall the clan. Not wanting to be the only ones to voice their apprehensions they stayed silent. Instead, they peered around the headwaters looking for the perfect place to build the new dam. "This one will stop the flow of water into the pond and save the day," explained one of the leaders. Emin and Wakcu just listened. The beavers were so proud of themselves; they just knew everyone would want to celebrate their success. Not only were they going to create a wonderfully improved place to live, but they were going to be heroes! "We should keep this quiet 'til we're done," said the elder beavers. "Then we'll tell them what we've done and they won't have a chance to steal our glory."

So the beavers went about their work. They tore down trees, pulled out bushes, and cleared the land. Very shortly they had the dam built. It was a wonderful structure with sound walls made from some of the tallest timbers. After placing the final stick, the beavers watched the waters push up against the dam and run off into tributaries on either side, carrying all the unwanted water away from the pond. With great pride and triumph they swam downstream in the now rapidly diminishing flow of water, returning to the pond and their beloved home. After finally stopping the water, Emin and Waku looked at each other as if defeated. What could they do? For Emin and Wakcu it was a quiet, cheerless swim home.

Six

*"What was it like when you
were young?"*

Within a few weeks of the dam's completion, a large number of dead fish appeared along the shoreline. The seagull swarms that savagely fed on the dead fish began to increase. Soon seagull droppings and dead fish began to foul the ground and the water. "This place isn't what it used to be," said the muskrats. "We used to love it here. The water was good and the neighbors friendly, but no more!" Fearing for the health of their children, the muskrats and mink reluctantly decided to move and go in search of a new home where the fish were healthy and the seagulls less annoying.

Soon the turtles too packed up their shells after noticing a decline in small fish and the water's dropping oxygen level. The turtles knew their lives depended on new broods of fish, so they waited until dark and slowly began their move. Like many of the animals, they moved to a neighboring pond created by the dam's diverted waters.

As the water became stagnant, weeds began to fill the pond. The oxygen levels continued to dip and even more small fish disappeared. The combination of weeds and lowered oxygen levels now failed to allow the sunlight to filter down into the water.

The beavers, now alarmed by the quality of life at the pond, began arguing amongst themselves, looking for someone to blame. "No one else wants to do anything," complained an elder. "We can't get anyone to help. We even sat in our dams waiting for the other animals to help us find a solution, but when we called, no one came."

Several beavers had begun talking with Emin and Wakcu. Distrust continued to develop and conversations between the original beavers and the new-thinking beavers became less and

The Pond

less frequent. Secretly the two different groups began talking about and watching each other; feeling that if the other animals left, then it would be just a matter of time before they were left with all the work. They began talking in small groups when they were outside their dens, rather than openly sharing information inside the dens. On one outing, a few of the beavers from both groups were out looking for young saplings. They had brought some of the younger cubs out with them to teach them the art of selecting the softest and most nourishing saplings from amongst the forest floor.

As they walked, they talked about the others, crying how they couldn't trust each other any more and how so much had changed. "What was it like in the old days?" asked one cub. "What was it like when you were young?" The eldest beaver stopped in his tracks and stared at the younger beaver annoyed with the question. "What was it like?" he sarcastically responded. "Well it was a wonderful place!" As his face lost its anger, he almost began to smile. "It's not your fault," he said to the younger inquisitor. "I guess it just makes me mad that things have gotten to where they are," the older beaver continued. "But what was it was like?" the younger beaver pressed. The young cub desperately wanted to understand what was different before, for this new pond was all the younger beaver had ever known.

Well, the older beaver began to talk about the pond in its hay day, all it had offered, and what it felt like to be a part of the pond community. He went on for what seemed like a long time, when one of the other elders noted it was getting late and that they should be getting back to the huts before the others began to worry. As the elders began to lead the group back, they stopped and turned toward the youngsters. "Please don't tell anyone about what we talked about this evening, okay?" The younger beavers agreed but wondered what was so secretive about what they had heard. Yet they agreed and continued their hike back to the den. That night the elders slept the best they had in a long time while the young beavers quietly lay in their beds, dreaming about the pond they had only heard about.

Seven

*"Doing what we've always done before
isn't working!"*

For a long time nothing more was said about the stories the beavers had heard that day. However, several weeks later a huge argument developed over the fact that a few more beavers were quietly voicing their concerns about the new dam. Ophev, an elder, had grown impatient with the underlying dissension caused by what he saw as a lack of enthusiasm from the forward thinkers. "No beaver that respects the traditions of the mound, or respects himself, would ever disagree with decisions made by the Council!" he exclaimed. Ophev had come into power when a tree he was cutting had accidentally fallen on their former leader. Ophev was young and the strongest beaver at the time and no one was willing to question his request to the Council to take charge. He had known that several of the beavers were unhappy about building the dam and the flood that resulted but he had ne¹ been questioned before and he was not about to let tradition, which had always provided the laws of the mound, be questioned. "Silence is better than questions" was his motto and he had never had any doubt that the others believed this as well. After all, why would they? No leader he knew of had ever been questioned.

Emin, already frustrated from the dam-building incident, spoke up to Ophev. "We can't keep doing this! Doing what we've always done before isn't working! The pond's continuing to get worse and unless we try something new, this place will be no better than a swamp!" It was one of the most dishonoring things Emin could have said, which may have been the cause of the resulting name-calling session. Finally, after many nasty words were exchanged, the like-thinking beavers declared that it was time to branch off on their own and build a new mound a short distance from the central mound. The evening ended with a lot of crying and hurt feelings. But the next day, the like-thinking beavers set about building a new mound, only a stone's throw away from their original home.

Eight

*"At what point did the pond
begin to change?"*

In their new home the beavers felt safe and began talking amongst themselves more openly. Soon the younger beavers began feeling secure enough to ask about the early days of the pond, and lengthy discussions ensued. The more the elder beavers talked about the old pond, the more excited they became. They began drawing pictures for the younger beavers to help them understand what their home had looked like before the storm, and soon the cubs were asking to visit specific parts of the pond.

One of the first places they wanted to visit was the upper part of the pond where the beavers had built their dam at the pond's peak. The younger beavers were amazed to see the fantastic dam that had been build "just before the pond changed," as one of the older beavers described it. It was a marvelous piece of construction and would last forever. The younger beavers were left awestruck by what they'd seen, but the older beavers were only more confused. That night, after the kids were asleep, the beavers cautiously talked about their trip. Emin silently sat back listening to the conversation. As usual, he was quick to listen and slow to talk, but when he said something, he stood behind it and tonight was no exception.

There was a lull in the conversation when Emin quietly broke the silence. "At what point did the pond begin to change?" he asked. "Doesn't it seem strange that the dam was built at the same time that the pond started to change for the worse? Do you think there's a connection between the dam and the changes in the pond?" he mused. The other beavers couldn't believe what he was asking. "Dam building is what we do!" they exclaimed, admonishing Emin for his rude remark. "How can you question our very purpose? It is what we do and what we've always done!" they exclaimed.

Emin, not knowing if he should go on or be quiet figured he was in enough trouble already so he continued. "We moved into this mound because we wanted to do things differently, right?" he asked. The other beavers slowly and sheepishly looked down and then at each other. "Yes, that's right," one finally spoke, "but does that give us the right to question what we've always done?" "Well we moved here because we didn't like what was happening over there, right?" Emin shot back. "Yes," they reluctantly responded. "And we would be just like them if we continued to do what they were doing, right?" Emin continued. The other beavers seemed to begin to agree. "If we are willing to talk about what we think, even if it doesn't make sense, we might find a better way of doing things," Emin paused. The other beavers began nervously talking amongst themselves. Emin sat back, knowing they would need a little time to discuss what they were thinking. In his heart Emin knew they were finally on the right track.

After a fairly long discussion, the beavers settled down and sat back in what seemed to be quiet acceptance. After a long while, one of the middle-aged beavers spoke up, "I think you're right, Emin. For years we have walked on duck eggs to appease the other beavers. It's time we said what's on our minds." He paused, looking around the room, "The first thing we need to do is agree to do everything we can to be honest with each other, and ourselves. I think it's not being honest that's hurt us in the past. Maybe if we'd been more honest with each other, we wouldn't be living in separate huts." The beavers all nodded in agreement. Then Emin spoke up, "We don't need to blame anyone. We just need to begin talking about what we really think and want." With that the den began to buzz with excitement, small side conversations breaking out throughout the den.

"Remember how we use to surprise the deer by splashing them when they came for their early morning drink?" one beaver reminisced. "And remember how we'd race from one end of the pond to another?" chimed in another. As they began to tell stories of their past lives at the pond, the younger beavers sat there, thrilled by the stories and at the same time, taken aback by the adults who were suddenly acting so strange. They liked what was happening, but they weren't sure what exactly it was. Some of the young beavers began speaking amongst themselves about how they were uncomfortable with all of the changes occurring. As the older beavers noticed the young beavers become concerned, they invited the younger beavers to share their thoughts, and for the first time they truly listened as these new concerns were shared.

Another older beaver named Zed, who was self-proclaimed one of the strongest swimmers, shared his fear that the younger beavers' ideas might slow their progress. Emin gently reminded him of their new desire to be honest, "I know you're concerned with the changes we're making, but if we want to be honest and hear everyone, then we have to hear it all!" Zed agreed and explained to the group just what it was that he feared. Many of the beavers admitted that they also felt like Zed but had been afraid to speak up. When they had finished, everyone began to understand the value of listening and voicing their fears and concerns, as well as their excitement with what was happening. This seemed to even further ignite the enthusiasm within the group and they spoke late into the evening. The beavers decided to record all the ideas they voiced so they would remember them. They also chose which ideas they would take on now and which they would try later. It was important that all the ideas be heard and written down; if a beaver was willing to put their ideas out there, then they were important enough to be written down.

Nine

*"It's not about being right or wrong,
but about working to improve what we
have."*

The beavers discovered that the ideas that they at first thought were the silliest or the most outrageous were actually the ideas that created the most valuable thoughts. Besides that, it allowed them to laugh and have fun. They also learned that every beaver experienced pain and endured struggle. And if they could find time to laugh, it made so many things that much better.

As they practiced generating ideas, their trust grew. As they grew, some beavers discovered that they were good listeners. In fact, they learned that each of them had a different skill and a unique experience to draw from. Sharing made their spirit, as well as their pride, soar.

The beavers spoke about how great it was to be able to say whatever came to mind, and feel safe enough to say it without being afraid of rejection. They learned how important it was to support each other, knowing that some day they would be supported. As the beavers' trust in each other grew, each grew as an individual. Challenging common wisdom or previously sacred beliefs became more commonplace. It was done with the utmost respect; recognizing that everything that is done, is done because the beaver doing it truly believed it was the best thing to do at that time. They also began to recognize the value in asking hard questions; the questions that so many beavers had been afraid to ask before—the questions that the beavers had been expected not to ask. You see, some of the middle-aged beavers had remembered hearing about a time when beavers were land dwellers. In fact, it was not until wolves began attacking that they moved their homes out into the water. This could mean that if the beavers had not initially changed their ways of thinking, beavers might have become extinct. Knowing the truth, they learned the value in the wisdom of the past, and that by asking questions they could decide how much of a prior belief still applied and what they could try different.

The beavers began talking about past decisions and if those decisions had resulted in making the pond a better, more vibrant place. Within a few days, they decided to try to recreate some of the things that were happening when the pond was vibrant. After reviewing the decisions that had most recently been made, the beavers decided to go up to the headwaters and open the dam a bit. They knew the pond needed fresh water despite the fact that their actions would anger those from the original mound. So the beavers made their way to the dam. As soon as they opened the dam the tiniest bit, fresh water flowed into the pond. One of the older beavers stopped to take in a large breath of fresh air. "It has been a long time since I've smelled the wonderful scent of new water." The young beavers immediately dove into the fresh new pool before them. They found the fresh water stimulated their skin and made their fur smooth. They weren't sure they liked the movement of the water, but they kept in mind that when they had previously experienced change, it wasn't always comfortable. After a few minutes, the beavers swam back to their mound and climbed on top to watch the water slowly refill the pond. The water ever so slowly began to rise as Emin came out of the mound and saw the water level climbing. He voiced his concern of the waters rising too fast and suggested they lower the dam on their end of the pond so the water wouldn't flood their home. The beavers agreed that this sounded like a reasonable request so they began to lower the level of the dam. After only a short period of time, the water began to stabilize and the beavers cheered.

With all the commotion outside, several of the beavers from the original mound came out to see the water level rising. "What happened?" they asked. "We decided to change the dam," replied one of the young beavers. "Are you out of your minds?!" an original mound beaver yelled. "You are ruining everything! Beavers are supposed to build dams, not tear them down! If you were to do anything, you should have built it up more! Not tear it down! That's what we've always done!" The beavers from the original mound were clearly upset, yelling at the new mound dwellers but the beavers just wouldn't listen.

For the next few nights, the original mound dwellers would sneak out at night and build the dam back up, but the next morning the new mound dwellers would tear it back down. Tensions between the two groups were clearly at a breaking point, but the older mound dwellers simply would not talk about it. Meanwhile, the new mound dwellers openly discussed what they wanted to create. They listened to the wisdom of their elders and the fresh perspectives of the young, weighing their options in order to select the best possible choice.

Two days later, a few of the younger beavers were feeding on the some soft water lily shoots when they realized that some of the beavers from the original mound were swimming just on the other side of the water lilies. The older beavers were not aware of the young beavers' presence so the young beavers kept quiet, lowering themselves into the water amongst the weeds so as to not to be seen. They silently listened to the older beavers speak as they swam. "It's been a long time since I felt the refreshing flow of new water in this place," one said. "I know," said another, "I don't want to admit it, but the smell of dead fish is almost gone too...maybe the change wasn't such a bad thing for the pond after all." The young beavers could hardly keep themselves quiet as the beavers swam away.

Once the older beavers were out of sight, the younger beavers swam as fast as they could to their den. As soon as they were inside, the beavers started yelling, unable to contain themselves. "They admitted they were wrong!" yelled the youngster. "We were right and they were wrong! We were right and they were wrong!" they began to chant. Hearing the chants, Emin came out to meet them. The young beavers were clearly excited but Emin took them aside. "I know you're excited about what you heard," he said, "but it's important to remember that it was those very beavers who kept this pond going for generations. It's not about being right or wrong, but about working to improve what we have. Putting them down fails to honor all they've done and we need to respect their experience. Remember how hard it was when we first started to talk amongst ourselves? Well, we need to give them a chance to learn as well. We all learn at a different pace, so we have to let them learn at theirs." The little beavers looked down, feeling a bit embarrassed of their gloating. But Emin continued, "It is great that they're seeing the good in this though, isn't it?" He smiled and winked at the young beavers, letting them know that while they too were learning, it was okay to be proud of the changes.

Later that night the beavers in the new mound brought up the history and experience of the original members. They also discussed what the two young beavers had overheard at the pond earlier. They felt encouraged by the fact that maybe, just maybe, the other beavers were starting to see the good in what they had done. The beavers began to debate potential action plans. The forward thinkers wanted to give the others an opportunity to hear why it was they left the original mound, and more importantly, why they had tried something new. Unfortunately the original mound members were notorious for being closed minded and unable to talk openly. But the beavers knew they needed to know more about the elders' experiences, good and bad, so they could continue to improve the pond. They needed to learn from them and try to show them that they not only meant well but they also had proof that trying something new can work. Most importantly though, they knew they'd have to work together to make that happen.

This discussion prompted them to invite the old mound dwellers to their next meeting. Emin himself was selected to go to the original mound to deliver the invitation. He knew this wouldn't be an easy task, but he'd received lots of advice from his new community. The beavers encouraged Emin to expect a positive reaction from the meeting. They had found that when they expected bad things to happen, they often did. But when they anticipated positive results, they tended to get a positive result. Not being stupid, they practiced what they had learned and that was to expect the best! The beavers asked Emin to invite the original mound dwellers to share their experiences and concerns with them so they could honor what the beavers had done and come to understand it.

The beavers also told Emin that they supported him no matter what happened. Knowing this took a lot of the pressure off Emin and allowed him to use his best judgment. He knew his primary goal was to be kind and to work for increased understanding. As long as Emin was clear about what was expected of him, he knew what to do and it would be okay. But despite his desire to approach the mound with a positive mind, he was nervous and extremely glad to have the support of his community. He knew that if it didn't work, his mound would still support him. Making mistakes was acceptable, so long as they were willing to learn from it. Without the ability to safely take risks, the chance for change was not likely. They were trying things no other beaver had tried before and they knew it would take a lot more effort.

When Emin finally approached the mound, Ophev suspiciously greeted him at the door. "What are you doing here?" he asked. "I want to invite you and the others to meet with us. I know we don't agree on what to do with the pond so I'm asking you to give us a chance to try to understand your thinking. You have a great deal of wisdom we can learn from and it would be an honor if you would come. Will you please agree to come to the meeting?" Ophev was a bit taken aback by the request. He was skeptical of why exactly he was being invited. Yet in spite of his hesitation, his curiosity outweighed his reluctance. "All right," he said, "We'll come." Then after a moment's pause he continued, "Who exactly should come?" "Anyone can come who wants to," Emin replied. "We want to open our minds to all the information we can get. The more information we have, the better decisions we can make." Ophev didn't know what to do with the openness of the invite but he was afraid not to accept the invitation. He just had to know what they were up to.

Ten

*"The more information we have, the
better decisions we can make."*

The next day the entire community
from the original mound showed up
to meet with the new mound members. A
large sign had been placed on the front of the
mound to announce their arrival. And as the
beavers began to arrive one by one, they were
each greeted at the doorway. They were very
cautious at first but quickly found themselves
at home. Ophev was again taken aback by the
the warm welcoming. He cautioned those near
him to be wary of their tricks, but the beavers
felt very much at home as they were welcomed

with the offering of fresh shoots to nibble on as they were shown around the new mound. Once everyone had a chance to become familiar with the new surroundings, a young beaver, a middle-age beaver, and an elder beaver each performed a formal welcome presentation for the visitors. The beavers then invited their guests to open the discussion.

Immediately, Ophev stood and asked why they were there. "We certainly appreciate that you wanted to show us your mound...show us what a wonderful new home you've created for those who abandoned us, but what do you want from us?" he asked angrily.

The new mound beavers were not surprised by his question. "We realize a lot has caused where we are today," Emin said. But before he could continue, Ophev blurted out, "So that is it? You are here to blame us for everything that has happened! WE are certainly not to blame! We will soon be living in a swamp because of what YOU have done to the dam!" The original mound beavers seemed to become agitated by his remarks and a couple chimed in, "Is that what this is all about?" The new mound beavers seemed unfazed by the remarks, which angered Ophev even more. "Let's get out of here!" he shouted. But before the beavers could stand, Emin responded loudly, "We didn't bring you here to blame you." And then in a quite and reassuring tone he continued. We invited you here so we could tell you we are sorry for everything that has happened and we want to extend you a branch of understanding." The visiting beavers were shocked by this overture and silence overtook the mound. Quietly, one of the smallest of the beavers carried out a branch and laid it in front of Ophev. It was a branch from a white birch tree, the sacred sign, symbolizing the end of a major conflict or struggle.

The legend of the birch tree tells a story of a beaver who was seriously wounded fighting the beaver's mortal enemy, the wolf. This beaver had been able to outsmart the wolf in order to save his mound. He tricked the wolf into following him into the water where the wolf, unable to swim, drowned. However, in the process, the beaver was badly wounded and left bleeding. As the legend goes, the beaver dragged himself over to the dark brown birch tree and fell against it, lying at the foot of the tree, dying. The tree, being made of the same life force as the beaver, saw the beaver and took pity on him. Knowing that there wasn't much time, the tree quickly did the only thing it could. It allowed the "color of life" to drain out of its roots and into the beaver, saving his life. The beaver began to regain his strength and eventually was able to return to his mound. From that day forward, the birch tree has

remained white.

With the white branch at his feet, Ophev finally realized that Emin and the forward thinkers were serious. The gift of the branch expressed their intentions far better than any words. Waku spoke up, "We want to understand you. I know we think differently, but I want… we want to understand what you think, what you believe, and to hear the stories of the things that have made your mound happy, healthy, and wise." With these words the older mound members listened and began to smile. Maybe they really were on the same page after all. "We believe you want what's best for the pond, and our children, just as we do. But we need your help. Tell us what it was like when you were young and the pond was vibrant!"

Excitement seemed to flourish and the original mound dwellers, one by one, began to reach out and share their stories and memories of the pond. For hours the stories came to life and as they spoke, the energy changed. The beavers talked long into the night, and as the sun began to rise, Emin invited everyone to retreat to their perspective mounds to rest and think about all they had discussed. Beavers from each mound hugged each other as they parted. Last to leave was Ophev. He and Emin met at the door. "I'm not sure what happened here tonight," Ophev said, "but thank you for inviting us." Emin watched him as he walked away. "I don't think he's sold," Emin said aloud to no one in particular, "but I know I am." And with that he smiled as he went over to his soft mat to lie down. It was late in the morning before there was any sign of the beavers on the pond that day.

Eleven

"Listening became most important and those who typically had all the answers now realized the value of being silent."

Over the next few months, the conversation between mound members increased. With tensions lowered and the pond returning to a more nurturing setting, the animals slowly began to return. The young learned from their elders but shared in recreating the pond into the home they collectively wanted. Stories were shared and actions compared to prevent them from repeating mistakes of the past.

The animals learned from each other and their different points of view. With each story they heard from a different animal culture the more their problem-solving skills improved, and more diverse options created. Listening became most important and those who typically had all the answers now realized the value of being silent. A gentle calm settled over the pond and everyone was comforted as they learned their role, what was expected of them, and where they were going as a community. The beavers were finally making the pond a better place, rather than the place it had always been.

Then one morning Ocheoh, one of the younger beavers, woke Emin from a deep sleep, shaking him. "What is it?" Emin asked. "You've got to see this!" Emin quickly rubbed the sand from his eyes and ducked out the door behind the young beaver. He followed the beaver to the top of the mound where they could see a couple of the beavers from the original mound in the distance, slowly kicking, as if by accident, sticks off the top of the dam. "What do you think they're doing?" asked Ocheoh. Emin didn't dare speculate, but he'd come to know the signs of change. "I'm not sure," he said quietly, "but I think it's gonna be good." The young beaver looked at Emin inquisitively but Emin just smiled.

Several years later, a young boy and his father were walking through the woods when they came upon a beautiful pond. They paused at the shoreline for a few moments while the father told his son about the many hours of fishing he had done at this very spot. "It used to be a beautiful place..." he trailed off and then started again, "but it seems to be even more beautiful now than I remember." The father looked reminiscently at his place of youth, then he turned to his son and said, "Why don't we see if we can find a place to fish right here?" And with that the duo walked the edge of the crystal waters, fishing poles in hand, looking for the perfect spot to fish.

John K Kriger   72

Epilogue

What can we learn from the pond?

The pond serves as a metaphor for the way many organizations function. The pond operates like the environments we work and live in, while the animals represent the members within our organizations: our colleagues, our families, and even ourselves. Each of the animals attempts to do what they think is best; however, each member consequently reacts from a different perspective, set of values, vision, and capability. Yet, they are often unaware of these differences and assume to know what others are thinking.

1

In the pond, the wildlife found food, protection, and a social structure to meet their needs. In organizations people can also be fed in many ways: socially, emotionally, physically, and spiritually. Sometimes organizations provide actual food or other simple needs. Sometimes it is feeding them information. Other times feeding is offering the support they don't get outside of meetings, and sometimes, it's the security of having a place they feel welcome; to quote the old TV show *Cheers*, a "place where everybody knows your name." Meeting the basic needs of the members of any organization is important to overall achievement. Psychologist Abraham Maslow constructed the hierarchy of needs to describe the fact that we can't achieve higher level needs until we have satisfied our most basic needs. We can't seek belonging until our physical needs of safety, food, and shelter are met. Once the basic needs are satisfied, we can think about joining, achieving, and finding balance in our efforts. At first the pond met basic needs so higher levels of achievement could be addressed.

2

The animals wanted so much to continue having a peaceful environment that they failed to resolve the problems with which they were confronted. Because of their fears, they failed to get the assistance and information they needed. They loved the pond the way it "was." The problem was that what had been, no longer existed. As soon as they realized what is was that they liked, it changed. What was, was constant and subtle change; change that is required for everything to be maintained. Water needs to flow and constantly be refreshed. Members need to learn new information and adapt to the changes occurring. Denying the existence of change instead contributes to negative change and passively allows it to happen. Wanting to maintain the "status quo" kept the animals quiet; rather than addressing the changes, they "suffered in silence." If the animals had accepted the changes that were occurring, they might have taken the risk to speak openly of their fears. Honest information is often difficult to get, but it can be harder to hear. Had the beavers received a wider perspective, they might have responded rather than reacted.

The Pond

Gathering new information would have also helped the animals better establish and, consequently, fulfill their purpose. The beavers instead wanted to hang on to their current beliefs and behaviors. They tried to hang on to the past rather than creating future goals. As you read these words, the fact that you have read them creates something in the past, and not the thoughts of your future. Living for the future is one thing, living in it is another.

3

Further clouding the issue was the fact that the beavers acted to keep the pond the same without first assessing it. They didn't think to examine what positives they could keep, which might have better guided their efforts. Instead, the beavers reacted without knowing where they were going, and fear is never a good source of guidance. This is especially true with proactive planning, which should be done before problems arise.

The beavers also failed to note that the pond was a dynamic environment. If they had, the beavers would have known that the only consistent thing you could count on in a dynamic environment is change. Change happens! Recognizing the potential for change, and planning for it, counteracts the tendency toward denial. When change is embraced, and there is a plan to work within it, the very power of the change itself will propel us forward.

The Pond

4

Neither the beavers, nor the other animals ever stated what it was they wanted from the pond. They knew what they didn't want, but they never created a clear vision of what they did. As it often happens, the beavers worked to stop change rather than work toward a goal. If the beavers had realized that they'd get what they paid attention to, they might have worked harder on what was good in their environment. Even if the beavers had decided on a short-term goal, they might have been able to see if the actions they were taking were moving them toward or away from their goal.

Goals based on current assessment provide direction. Clearly defined community-created goals can unite diverse needs and provide consistent support. Once goals are determined, they are prioritized and sorted into short, intermediate, and long-term goals. The beavers failed to enlist the other animals or work with them to create clear goals, and consequently their efforts lacked direction. Involving the other animals and discussing what was important to each would have offered them options based on the entire pond community's values.

5

The pond provided rich resources for growth and development. When the resources decreased, discomfort followed. In the human world resources are often perceived as financially dependent, when in reality there is a lot that does not depend on funding. In fact, it is amazing what happens when people, or in this case animals, talk to each other and share resources. The small fish and frogs could safely swim because they were utilizing the resource of safety to their benefit. What around us is not being used? How many of us have a substantial number of others around us, supporting us, playing with us, and helping us? Or are we like the animals, learning to distrust, withdraw, and shut ourselves off from the rest of the "herd?" Shared resources enhance the capacity of everyone involved. This is known as "synergy." Synergy creates a greater result than any resource or talent separately. In fact, the synergistic effect enhances the group's efforts. The wildlife, water, and plants created an ecosystem capable of sustaining life, resulting in an environment of beauty, substance, and wonder. Like the pond, organizations can become magical when their resources and assets match their needs.

The Pond

6

Success, or over reliance on past success, can often cloud judgment. Success can make us overconfident and complacent. We spend time patting ourselves on the back without looking behind us to see how it could have been even better. Success feels good but it can provide a false vision since success is what was, and not what is. Simply because we have succeeded does not mean we will always succeed. Situations, priorities, resources, and the environment constantly change. While change is occurring, we too are changing. And while all too often we deny it, we must instead "Live life on life's terms." We need to show up and be willing to live life as it is, and not as we would like it.

7

Organizations often fail, or seriously underutilize, the power of symbolism to convey and maintain organizational values. Like the creation of Post-it Notes from dog-eared hymnals, symbols and stories can carry meaning far beyond mere words. In the pond, the birch tree conveys the importance of an event, symbolizing the value of the intention of mending a broken relationship. Using the branch, the beavers quickly set the stage without a word, conveying a mission of clarity and hope to both sides. In many cases, this symbolism provided a context which words would otherwise fail to adequately express. Remember back when the flags were flown after the 9/11 attacks. For those who flew them, and those who merely saw them flying, the flags symbolized a sense of unity. They were a symbol of support toward those who acted when so many were immobilized by fear. Unlike words, a symbol can express many thoughts and ideals the very second it's displayed.

8

—∞∞∞—

Asking for the ideas of others would have provided the beavers with valuable insight. Without feedback, the beavers assumed everyone appreciated their actions despite not knowing the impact these changes had on the other animals and their environment. Failure to consider the pond's overall betterment further isolated the beavers. If the beavers had instead gained the animals' support, they may have provided options that they might not have otherwise considered. If we never ask, we most likely never find out. And if we do ask, sometimes we have to wait to get a valuable answer. When the beavers finally did ask, they didn't wait for an answer. Like the beavers, we often don't want know what's happening. But ignorance isn't bliss—it's dangerous! The beavers couldn't fix what they didn't know was happening. Because they didn't want to act, they didn't ask questions they didn't want answered. You need to ask yourself, are you truly willing to listen to those you are questioning?

9

It is interesting to see how easy it can be for someone outside the organization to see what's happening when often those on the inside can't. The father walking with his son was able to easily identify the changes and assess the pond's improvements. Blinded by the day-to-day activities, it can be easy to miss the subtle impact that changes create within our organization over time. Since there is often a lag between the subtle accumulation of change and the outcome, we fail to see the connection. The more immediate the results, the easier it is to connect our actions to the outcome. This is true even when we consider our lives. If you were to think about what brought you to your current place in life, it would be difficult to determine just what thought, what action, or what event brought you here. That is because it is the accumulation of thoughts, actions, and events that bring us to here. Numerous decisions and actions preempted the split between the beavers. Certainly some were affected more than others, but they all contributed to the end result. Would the forward-thinking beavers have taken such drastic action if the original mound members had not thought and acted as they had? While the exact tipping point can elude us, being aware of change as early as possible can greatly aid in our decision to continue on or change course.

Intentions executed without input lack balance, whereas external input provides unbiased feedback. If the beavers had heard an eagle's point of view, from their aerial perspective, they would have seen that their actions were actually creating negative, unintended results. But because the beavers were working under the premise of their good intentions, the other animals felt their skepticism and concern was unjustified. Consequently, resources that could have provided valuable insight into the impact of the beavers' actions, and a variety of alternatives, went unnoticed. Instead, the beavers moved with intention rather than knowledge. The beavers did have the best of intentions but intention, without direction, often fails to yield positive results. Without establishing a common goal for the pond community as a whole, the beavers were left without direction. They instead reacted, or lived by reactionary planning, rather than being proactive. Taking action, when direction and clarity are lacking, may alleviate a problem, or result in greater ones since viable options often go unexplored. Since the issue is not thought through expediency prevails and long term consequences are often not evaluated. In the case of the pond good intentions led the beavers to acts of ignorance, "If we're busy, we must be making a difference."

10

The beavers were not the only animals to change the pond. The other animals' conservative actions also contributed to the pond's demise. They failed to take action or to speak up when they observed things failing. At times it can be easier to blame others than to shoulder the reponsibility of improvement. Whether you don't want to look bad or just want to avoid confrontation, the outcome is often the same. A lack of action can have devastating consequences because, simply, nothing happens! The animals let their fear of being different and unpopular dictate their behavior. While certainly no one likes to be the problem in an organization, a healthy organization does require open and honest communication. Organizations can be a hot bed of disagreement and still be effective if they are working toward a common goal, if they all want more than to service their own interests. Dissent, for the purpose of improvement, can serve as a catalyst for honesty. Change for the better holds no room for sacred subjects or projects. The ability to ask questions is a cornerstone of self-assessment.

Organizations can also self-destruct over political and personal battles. An organization cannot be effective if it is more important to be on top than it is to meet the needs of the people whom the organization was formed to serve. If an organization's mantra is "we do it for the children," then this must be consistent from top to bottom. A functional organization must be consistent in words, values, actions, and intentions.

Trying to hold on to the present is like holding on to the current of the pond. By altering the natural processes of the pond's development, the beavers created the exact outcome they were trying to avoid. Fear of change caused them to take action in isolation, reducing their ability to seek information from the other animals. Fear caused the beavers to narrow their thinking and distrust others, becoming self-protective and suspicious of the other animals. As their trust diminished, so did their communication. The needs of the pond were ignored and the beavers became self-serving, further distancing themselves from the others.

When things change rapidly, the result of the change can often be more easily linked back to a particular action since there is a greater direct connection from the cause to the effect. However, when conditions change at such a slower pace, the beavers didn't notice the changes occurring, and more importantly, didn't associate their actions with the corresponding outcome. In the pond, each member offers a different energy, potential, and resource to the community. Like new information, fresh water, brings the beavers new energy, potential, concepts, and experiences. New water keeps the pond fresh and free from stagnation. Like the beavers, people all like to maintain what they feel is working. If a person continues to do what they have always done, they will likely get the same result. The pond was constantly changing with new members entering and leaving the environment. The weather changed and the seasons flowed creating a variation in resources, temperature, and climate. The pond's environment, at any given time, was changing for better or worse. So the beavers rationalized that if their efforts "could save just one beaver, then all of our efforts were worth it." But inadequate or mediocre efforts achieve minimal expectations. This approach dangerously justified the beavers' minimal efforts and inadequate planning. Creating an environment that meets the needs of all the pond animals would be an admirable goal. But although that vision was desired, the beavers accepted a significantly less optimal reality.

Wayne Dyer, in his PBS series *The Power of Intention*, says, " When you change the way you look at things, the things you look at change." It is not so much that we change things, but our willingness to see them from a different perspective changes. When we are satisfied with what we have and where we are, we stop looking, learning, and tend to close our minds. When we "intend" to grow and enhance our outlook, we expand our potential. This allows us to see farther than we have ever seen before, because we are standing on the "shoulders of our experience." We are using what we have done to see what we are capable of. However, we need to realize that greater balance is required the higher you go!

In the pond, small fry and larger predators all found a place and a purpose in their environment. Each served a purpose and had a place that was theirs to complete. Boundaries were clear but not ridged. There were times when the frogs were on land and there were times when they were in water. The pond did not keep them out when they left, but welcomed those seeking admission, without reservation, knowing that each held it's own special gifts to lend. Diversity enriched the culture of the pond, just as it enriches organizations. Organizations that learn to operate in functional ways become healthy and grow, while those, which are dysfunctional, tend to become more like swamps.

So ask yourself is your organization a thriving pond or a declining swamp? All organizations are either growing or in a state of decline. No organization stays the same for very long. And, more importantly, no organization is beyond improvement. The improvements may take time, attention, and hard work but to those willing to get their "fur ruffled" will find it well worth it. Working in a healthy and functional environment enhances the likelihood that members will stay, be more satisfied, and work more diligently to increase the capacity of the organization. Everyone benefits in a functional organization, even those in the wrong job or those who don't seem to fit in. Honesty helps us get the feedback that is often so hard to get. How many of us work in environments that really meet our needs? They are out there. If you don't happen to work in one, you can learn to create a more functional workplace. If you feel you can't create one, there are others out there for you to join and would welcome you and your talents. If you run an organization or business, you can gather feedback to find out what you can do to improve your organization so it offers its new and current inhabitants more opportunities for growth and enrichment. New, fresh, vibrant waters can constantly refresh your pond, offering resources, safety, and stimulation. Together you can create an environment like the pond that supports and encourages your employees, members, or colleagues, to move in, settle down, and stay because it's comfortable and their needs are met. Be well!!

If you are considering improving the function of your organization here are a few suggested resources useful in guiding, creating new thinking and to help you and your organization grow.

1. Cialdini, Robert B. Influence: Science and Practice. 4th ed. Needham Heights, MA: Allyn & Bacon, 2001.

2. Fritz, Robert. The Path of Least Resistance: Learning to Become the Creative Force in Your Own Life. New York, NY: Ballantine Books, 1989.

3. Gladwell, Malcolm. The Tipping Point. 1st ed. New York, NY: Little, Brown and Company, 2000.

4. Kotter, John P. Leading Change. Boston, MA: Harvard Business School P, 1996.

5. Senge, Peter M. The Fifth Discipline. New York, NY: Doubleday, 1990.

6. Yankelovich, Daniel. The Magic of Dialogue. New York, NY: Touchstone, 1999.

If you would like to improve the function of your "pond" or for further information on any of the programs and services provided by Kriger Consulting please contact us at www.krigerconsulting.com.

About the author

John K Kriger

As the President of Kriger Consulting, Inc., John K. Kriger provides organizational training, management consulting, assessment and evaluation services with his consulting team, throughout the United States and Bermuda. He is a Keynote Speaker and workshop presenter at numerous national and international conferences and on radio and television.

His extensive clients list includes corporations, national organizations, numerous federal, state, county, and local government departments, nonprofits, school districts, and universities, along with private and faith based organizations.

He holds a Bachelors degree in Human Services and a Masters of Science Degree in Management. John is a licensed Clinical Alcoholism and Drug Abuse Counselor, a Certified Prevention Specialist, a member of the American Society for Training and Development, and Toastmasters International. He lives in NJ with his wife and family.